A
Literature Unit
for

In the Year
of the
Boar
and
Jackie Robinson

by Bette Bao Lord

Written by Caroline Nakajima

Illustrated by Sue Fullam and Cheryl Buhler

Teacher Created Materials, Inc.

P.O. Box 1214

Huntington Beach, CA 92647

©1992 Teacher Created Materials, Inc.

Made in U.S.A.

ISBN 1-55734-417-5

Table of Contents

Introduction

A good book can touch our lives like a good friend. Within its pages are words and characters that can inspire us to achieve our highest ideals. We can turn to it for companionship, recreation, comfort, and guidance. It also gives us a cherished story to hold in our hearts forever.

In *Literature Units*, great care has been taken to select books that are sure to become good friends!

Teachers who use this unit will find the following features to supplement their own valuable ideas.

- Sample Lesson Plans

- Pre-reading Activities

- A Biographical Sketch and Picture of the Author

- A Book Summary

- Vocabulary Lists and Suggested Vocabulary Activities

- Chapters grouped for study, with each section including:
  - *quizzes*
  - *hands-on projects*
  - *cooperative learning activities*
  - *cross-curriculum connections*
  - *extensions into the reader's own life*

- Post-reading Activities

- Book Report Ideas

- Research Ideas

- A Culminating Activity

- Three Different Options for Unit Tests

- Bibliography

- Answer Key

We are confident that this unit will be a valuable addition to your planning, and hope that as you use our ideas, your students will increase the circle of "friends" that they can have in books!

Sample Lesson Plan

Each of the lessons suggested below can take from one to several days to complete.

Lesson 1

- Prepare students for the book by discussing background information. (See Pre-Reading Activities, page 7.)
- Read "About the Author" with your students. (page 5)
- Begin Reading Response Journals. (page 11)
- Introduce vocabulary words for Section 1. (page 8)
- Assign Word Detective worksheet (page 10) to be used while reading Section 1.

Lesson 2

- Read Chapters 1 and 2.
- Go over Word Detective worksheet and discuss meanings of words.
- Choose a vocabulary activity. (page 9)
- Discuss abacuses. Make one and learn how to use it. (pages 13 and 14)
- Make a map of the community and learn how to read it. (page 15)
- Discuss the differences between Shirley's homes in Chungking and Brooklyn. (page 16)
- Complete lesson on how to be "heard" by adults. (page 17)
- Administer Section 1 quiz. (page 12)
- Introduce vocabulary for Section 2. (page 8)
- Assign Word Detective worksheet for Section 2. (page 10)

Lesson 3

- Read Chapters 3 through 5.
- Go over Word Detective worksheet and discuss meanings of words.
- Choose a vocabulary activity. (page 9)
- Discuss cooking and recipes. (page 19)
- Talk about misunderstandings and how they affect us. (page 20)
- Examine expressions in the English language. (page 21)
- Write about being accepted. (page 22)
- Administer Section 2 quiz. (page 18)
- Introduce vocabulary for Section 3. (page 8)
- Assign Word Detective worksheet for Section 3. (page 10)

Lesson 4

- Read Chapters 6 through 8.
- Go over Word Detective worksheet and discuss meanings of words.

- Choose a vocabulary activity. (page 9)
- Discuss inventions and have students make their own. (page 24)
- Learn about the Brooklyn Dodgers and play game. (page 25)
- Discuss the Pledge of Allegiance. (page 26)
- Talk about doing things for others and make the coupons. (page 27)
- Administer Section 3 quiz. (page 23)
- Introduce vocabulary for Section 4. (page 8)
- Assign Word Detective worksheet for Section 4. (page 10)

Lesson 5

- Read Chapters 9 and 10.
- Go over Word Detective worksheet and discuss meanings of words.
- Choose a vocabulary activity. (page 9)
- Learn about Chinese horoscopes. (page 29)
- Discuss baseball cards and make individual cards. (page 30)
- Do the math problems. (page 31)
- Discuss loyalty and friendship. Assign acrostics. (page 32)
- Administer Section 4 quiz. (page 28)

Lesson 6

- Read Chapters 11 and 12.
- Review Shirley's experiences and make mobiles. (page 34)
- Discuss fables. Read *Chinese Zoo*. Write and perform fables. (page 35)
- Learn about Jackie Robinson and discuss other American contributors. (page 36)
- Discuss family heritage and do family tree project. (page 37)
- Administer Section 5 quiz. (page 33)

Lesson 7

- Assign book reports. (page 38)
- Assign research projects. (page 39)
- Begin culminating activity. (pages 40-42)

Lesson 8

- Administer Unit Tests 1, 2, and/or 3. (pages 43-45)
- Discuss test results and responses.
- Discuss the students' enjoyment of the book.

About the Author

The story of Bette Bao Lord's childhood is much like that of Shirley Temple Wong, the main character of *In the Year of the Boar and Jackie Robinson.* Lord was born in Shanghai, China, on November 3, 1938, the daughter of a Nationalist Chinese government official. She came to live in Brooklyn, New York at age eight. She enrolled at P.S. 8 and started school two years ahead of her chronological age because she counted her age as 10 years as is the traditional Chinese custom. Her size, compared to the other fifth graders, did not seem unusual since Chinese were known to be small. She knew no English but adjusted well and began her successful career in America. Lord is quoted on the book cover as saying, "Many feel that loss of one's native culture is the price one must pay for becoming an American. I do not feel this way. I think we hyphenated Americans are doubly blessed. We can choose the best of both."

Lord attended Tufts University and received her Bachelor of Arts degree in 1959. The following year she received her Master of Arts at Fletcher School of Law and Diplomacy. Lord's varied and interesting career includes working with the East-West Cultural Center at the University of Hawaii, the Fullbright Exchange Program in Washington, D.C., and the National Committee on United States-China Relations. She has also performed and taught modern dance in Geneva and Washington, D.C. Her marriage in 1963 to Winston Lord, who served in the White House and the State Department in the 1970's and later became the American ambassador to China, has kept her in touch with politics. They have two children — Elizabeth Pillsbury and Winston Bao. In 1964 Lord became a naturalized U.S. citizen, and in that same year she wrote her first book.

The first book, *Eighth Moon: The True Story of a Young Girl's Life in Communist China,* was about her younger sister, Sansan, who grew up in China and was reunited with her family after sixteen years. *Spring Moon: A Novel of China* was her next book and was nominated for the American Book Award in 1982. It is the story of a Chinese family's experiences during the dramatic cultural and political changes in China during the 20th century. *In the Year of the Boar and Jackie Robinson* is her first children's book and was written in 1984. In addition to being an ALA Notable Book, this work received the Jefferson Cup Award from the Virginia Library Association in 1985 and the Child Study Association of America's Children's Book of the Year in 1987.

In the Year of the Boar
and Jackie Robinson

by Bette Bao Lord
(Harper Trophy, 1984)
(Available from Harper Collins in Canada, U.K. and Australia)

It is the beginning of 1947 and a young Chinese girl named Sixth Cousin, whose nickname is Bandit, is living happily with her family and all her relatives in the House of Wong. Her father has gone away to seek his fortune, and finally, after a year of absence, he sends a letter asking his wife and daughter to join him in Brooklyn, New York. Although sad to leave her relatives and homeland, she is excited about the prospect of moving to the United States. In honor of her new life in America, Grandfather announces that Bandit must be given a new and proper American name. Limited in her knowledge of American names, Bandit chooses the only one she knows other than Uncle Sam, Shirley Temple.

Shirley soon learns that life in America is quite different from her life in Chungking. She is amazed by the structures and "machines" of convenience, such as the ice box, stove, and washing machine. Not only did things look different, but she had to learn a completely new way of doing things.

Not knowing the language and customs of Americans leads to some humorous misunderstandings, but it also is the cause of her loneliness. Eventually, Shirley overcomes those initial barriers and develops new friendships. By the end of the year, she has learned about the sport of baseball and the great player, Jackie Robinson, who becomes her hero. Through him, Shirley comes to understand what it means to be an American, to strive to be the best that one can be, and to be able to make a difference for the betterment of society.

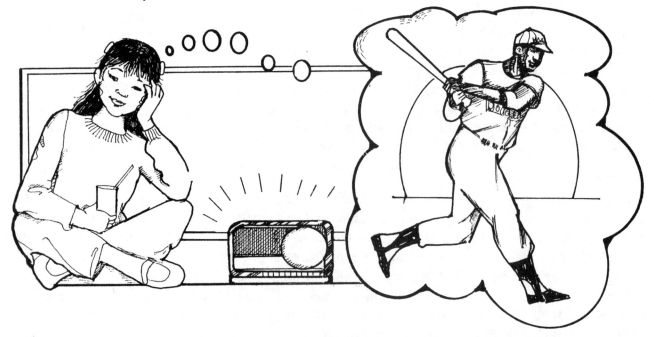

Before the Book

To introduce the book, *In the Year of the Boar and Jackie Robinson*, you may want to simply ask students what they think the title means. Questions that may help stimulate responses may include:

- Who was Jackie Robinson?

- What is he best known for?

- What is the meaning of Year of the Boar?

- Where might the term come from?

Depending on the prior knowledge of your students, it may be helpful to supply the background information yourself in order to prepare them for the story.

- Explain that in China and other Asian countries, there are 12 animals which "rule" a given year, always in a specific order. The year's events and people born in that year are believed to be influenced by the characteristics of the year's animal. This story takes place during one of the years belonging to the Boar.

- The Dodgers, who are now playing in Los Angeles, used to play in Brooklyn, New York.

- Jackie Robinson was a great baseball player who played for the Brooklyn Dodgers. He was the first black person to play on a major league team.

- This is the story of a young Chinese girl who comes to live in America in 1947. She must learn to be an American by learning a new language and new customs, while maintaining her own cultural heritage.

Given the background information, ask students to make some predictions.

- Will the girl be successful?

- What is the connection between her and Jackie Robinson?

- Will this be a happy or sad story?

- What problems might she encounter?

Vocabulary Lists

On this page are vocabulary lists which correspond to each sectional grouping of chapters. Vocabulary activity ideas can be found on page 9 of the book.

Section 1
Chapters 1-2

patriarch	unperturbed	extravagant
brazier	cringe	solemn
scurried	queasiness	irate
matriarch	torrential	jostled
plaited	dapper	abacus
dictums	mocking	ogled
squandered	mettle	mourners
ignorant	festooned	replica
kaleidoscope	queried	courtesans
skeptical	melodious	emphatic
writhed	utterly	faltered
rebuke	mishap	

Section II
Chapters 3-5

ambassador	eked	custom
dregs	trifle	grimaced
escapade	ordeal	protruded
compelling	revolted	balmy
elaborate	gossamer	sidling
sashay	forlorn	reverent
pelting	kow-tows	humiliated
regale	illustrious	formidable
hoary	intimidated	odious
devour	sinister	feeble
billowing	interrogate	fleetingly

Section III
Chapters 6-8

beckoned	spruce up	ritual
tyranny	etched	coaxed
disarming	unearthed	proposal
alchemy	fraught	ingenuity
timbre	transmuted	hostility
adept	awkwardly	meticulous
desolate	collided	lure
befitted	mayhem	vermin
plague	callously	sultry
ousted	disposition	ancestral

Section IV
Chapters 9-10

concoction	bribery	equivalent
deposit	frantically	aspire
composure	essence	progressives
counterfeit	recitation	crucial
berserk	ritual	chamber music
seizure	scurrying	amateurs
prolonged	walloping	indistinguishable
banished	emanated	phenomenon

Section V
Chapters 11-12

commemorate	feigned
reunion	swoon
toiling	futility
elixir	embarked
hovered	sterling
filial	dappled
resources	shimmering

Vocabulary Activity Ideas

Here are some activities that can be used to help your students learn and retain the vocabulary in *In the Year of the Boar and Jackie Robinson*.

❏ Find the sentence in the book with the given vocabulary word. Copy it. Rewrite the sentence by **Substituting a Synonym** which would make sense. The worksheet on page 10 may be used for this activity.

❏ Ask your students to make their own **Crossword Puzzles** or **Wordsearch Puzzles** using the vocabulary words from the story. Have them exchange papers and work the puzzle. When completed, the authors can correct the papers.

❏ Make up sentences for each word, but leave the word out. Trade papers and have the partner **Fill in the Blanks.**

❏ **Fictionary** can be played as a way of introducing new vocabulary. Establish small groups of 4 to 6 people. You will need note paper of uniform size and color. Someone in the group becomes "IT." IT writes down the correct definition of a word from the dictionary on a slip of paper, plus a fictional definition on another slip of paper. Each group member makes up a possible definition and writes it on a slip of paper. Try to make all the definitions sound official. IT collects and shuffles all the definitions. Then IT reads the definitions and the other group members must guess the correct definition. IT receives one point for each group member he/she successfully "stumps," and group members are awarded one point for guessing the correct definition. Play then moves to the next person on the left to be IT.

❏ Use the words and definitions to play **Bingo.** Fold an 8 ½" X 11" (22 cm x 28 cm) paper into 16 squares. Have students randomly write the words chosen for this activity in each space. The caller reads a definition and the players mark the correct word. Markers can be pieces of cut index cards, beans, or raisins. The first person to cover a row, column, or diagonal calls out Bingo and is the winner.

❏ Play **Hangman** using the definition as a clue. This might be a good activity to be played in partners.

❏ Challenge your students to a **Vocabulary Bee!** This is similar to a spelling bee, but in addition to spelling each word correctly, the game participants must correctly define the words as well.

❏ Challenge your students to use a specific vocabulary word from the story at least **10 Times In One Day**. They must keep a record of when, how, and why the word was used!

❏ As a group activity, have students work together to create an **Illustrated Dictionary** of the vocabulary words.

❏ Play **20 Clues** with the entire class. In this game, one student selects a vocabulary word and gives clues about this word, one by one, until someone in the class can guess the word.

❏ Play **Vocabulary Charades.** In this game, vocabulary words are acted out!

Word Detective

For each vocabulary word, hunt through the section in the book for the word and copy the sentence in which you find it on the first line. Then, on the second line, rewrite the sentence using a synonym or phrase that would make sense and keep the same meaning.

Word	Sentence
	1. _____ _____ 2. _____ _____
	1. _____ _____ 2. _____ _____
	1. _____ _____ 2. _____ _____
	1. _____ _____ 2. _____ _____

Reading Response Journals

As your students read through *In the Year of the Boar and Jackie Robinson,* have them keep a Reading Response Journal. Reading journals are a wonderful way for students to make the personal connections that reading literature is all about. Here are a few ideas to help them along in their responses.

To create the journal, have students assemble lined and unlined paper in a cover. The cover can be a simple 12" X 18" (30 cm x 46 cm) piece of construction paper folded in half, or it can be made more sophisticated by using a regular report cover found in stationery stores. They may want to draw a design for the cover or simply title it and add their names.

Tell students that the purpose of the journal is for them to record their reactions, feelings, ideas, observations, and questions that come up as they read the story. They might want to copy a favorite sentence or key passage.

You may want to provide questions or relevant topics for students to respond to in order to stimulate writing. For example:

Section 1: What do you think it would feel like to leave the people and places with which you are familiar and move to a new place? Has anything like that happened to you?

Section 2: Do you think Shirley did the right thing about not telling anyone about what Mabel did? How would you have handled it?

Section 3: Sometimes people just need a little help to be able to accomplish something, like Shirley with baseball or Señora Rodriguez with her apartments. Tell about a time when someone helped you out.

Section 4: Who is your best friend? Why do you get along?

Section 5: Do you have a hero? Who is it and what do you admire about that person?

Sometimes students may want to respond to their reading by drawing a picture instead of writing. Have them use the blank pages to do so.

Tell them that they may share their responses with their classmates if they wish. Sharing is a great way to stimulate discussions and broaden points of view.

Emphasize that they will not be graded on grammar, punctuation, or spelling, but that effort is what is important.

Encourage students to expand their journal ideas into stories, essays, poems, and art displays.

Provide time for students to write in their journals daily.

Try to read journals regularly. Since emphasis is on content, not style or grammar, no corrections should be made. Respond by making non-judgmental and encouraging comments or asking questions such as, "That's an interesting idea!" or "Do you think you might want to have that happen to you?" If grades are given, they should be based on effort and number of entries.

Quiz Time!

1. What do you think the "ugly bald bird" on the stamp of Father's letter refers to?

   _____

2. How do Mother, Grandmother, and Grandfather react to the letter they receive?

   _____

3. Describe the traditional Chinese attitudes about recognizing people's opinions.

   _____

4. Why does Bandit believe that she is in deep trouble about the broken urn?

   _____

5. What misconceptions do Bandit's relatives have about America?

   _____

   _____

6. Name at least 3 Chinese New Year traditions.

   _____

   _____

   _____

7. Why does Bandit choose Shirley Temple as her new American name?

   _____

8. Where in the United States do Shirley and Mother go to meet Father, and how do they get there?

   _____

9. Describe at least 5 things Shirley sees in Brooklyn that are different from what she knew in Chungking.

   _____

   _____

   _____

10. What mishap occurs on Shirley's first day in Brooklyn?

   _____

   _____

Abacus

At the House of Wong, Shirley often heard Third Uncle clicking the beads on his abacus as he worked on his accounts. The abacus is a tool for counting and doing simple arithmetic. It is the forerunner of our modern calculators and computers. The abacus is still used around the world, with each country having its own name and style for it. In Japan the abacus, or soroban, is used in school beginning at about the third grade, and they even have an examination for obtaining an abacus operator's license. Proficient users can be faster than someone using an electric calculator!

In China the abacus is called suan-pan, which means counting tray. This Chinese abacus has rods with five beads below and two beads above a crossbar within a wooden or plastic frame. The beads on top are called the heaven beads and the lower ones are called the earth beads.

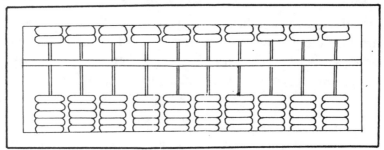

Make your own suan-pan and learn how easy adding and subtracting can be by using this simple number machine.

To make an abacus you will need:

    1 shoebox lid

    A strip of cardboard 1" (2.54 cm) wide and the length of the lid

    6 to 8 pieces of string at least 2" (5 cm) longer than the width of the lid

    Beads, "O" shaped cereal, or salad macaroni — 7 per string

    Tape

    Scissors

Tape the 1" strip of cardboard in a standing position inside the lid approximately 2" from one edge to create a horizontal divider for the beads.

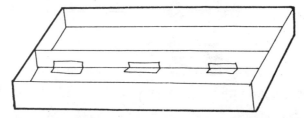

Cut six to eight ½" (1.3 cm) slits approximately 1" apart along the top and bottom edges and the cardboard divider. Then string 7 beads on each string, and place them into the slits so that 2 beads are above the divider and 5 are below. Tape the ends of the strings to the lid.

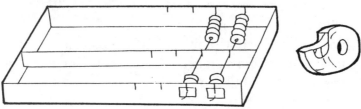

Abacus *(cont.)*

Now you are ready to use your new abacus. Each column of beads is like the "places" in our number system. The lower, or earth beads are each worth 1 and the upper, or heaven beads are each worth 5. Begin with all the beads moved away from the divider — heaven beads up and earth beads down. Choose any column to work with as the "ones" place. To show a number such as 3, simply move three earth beads up. To show the number 7, move one heaven bead down and two earth beads up.

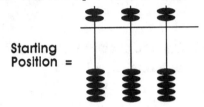 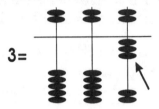 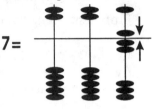

How do you think you would show the number 30? If you moved three earth beads up in the next column to the left, you are absolutely right! Which column would you use to show 300? Read the numbers on the picture abacuses below. Then try placing numbers 33, 77, 4, 146, 908, and 21 on your own abacus. (Be sure to clear your abacus between each number for this practice.)

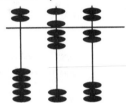 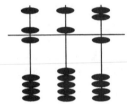 

Now let's try some simple arithmetic. To add 25 + 12, place 25 on the abacus. Then without clearing the beads, place 12 more. Look at the resulting number. Does it say 37?

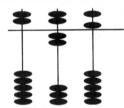 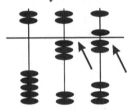

If at any time both heaven beads in a column are used up, just carry 1 earth bead up in the next column to take their place and clear those two heaven beads back away. For example, 7 + 5:

 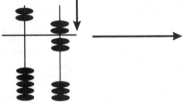 

To subtract, simply take away the second number of beads. Try 44 - 13. Your abacus should show:

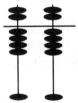

Try a variety of other addition and subtraction problems. 357 + 23; 1542 - 327; 48 - 21; 1679 + 274. Sometimes you may have to "borrow" from a higher column by exchanging a higher earth bead for two lower heaven beads to be able to do the subtraction.

In the Year of the Boar and Jackie Robinson

Maps

Poor Shirley could have used a map of her new neighborhood in Brooklyn that first day she arrived. With a map, she would have been able to see a picture of where she was and get home by herself.

There are all kinds of maps, and it is important to use the right kind to meet one's purpose. A map that shows the shape of the land, that is the hills, mountains, and valleys, is called a topographical map. It might show the heights of the ground using contour lines. The closer the lines are drawn, the steeper the hill. Another way of showing the shape of the land is called a relief map which can be shaded much like looking at a picture of it, or raised so that one can actually see the heights 3-dimensionally.

A road map is the type we are most familiar with because it is used when we are going someplace by car. It can be a small scale map that shows great distances and little detail or a large scale map that shows much detail within a small area. What kind of map did Shirley need?

Using a map of your school's attendance area, make an enlarged outline of the streets in your neighborhood. Cut the map into 4 quadrants and assign a part to each of 4 groups of students. Have each group add as many landmarks as possible to the map, such as schools, parks, stores, bus stops, trails, creeks, mailboxes, crosswalks, stop signs, etc. After putting the map back together, each person can make a small picture of his/her house, cut it out, and label it. Then play a game in which a student gives oral directions from the school to get to his/her house. Another student must follow the directions and pin the house in the correct location.

Here are some additional items you may want to add to the map:

1. compass indicating north, south, east, and west

2. scale showing the number of inches that equals one block

3. legend showing what the symbols mean

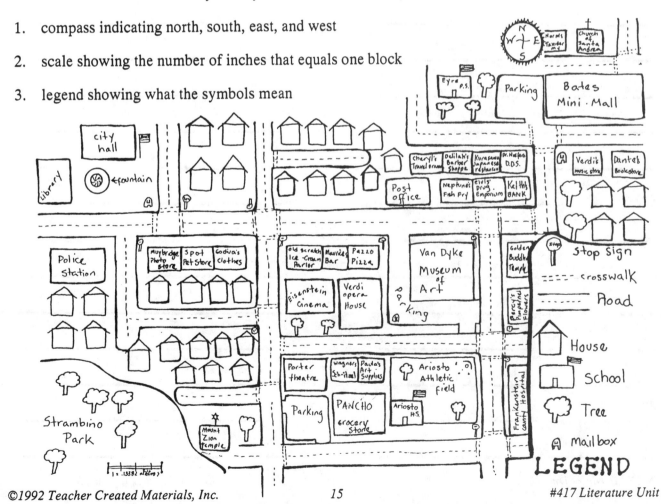

East Meets West

There were many differences between Shirley's homes in Chungking, China and Brooklyn, New York, both physically and culturally. Think about all the changes that Shirley encountered in moving to a new country and list them here. Some things to consider are:

landscape	structures	people
vehicles	activities	manners
home life	attitudes	family

Chungking, China   Brooklyn, New York

_____   _____

_____   _____

_____   _____

_____   _____

_____   _____

_____   _____

_____   _____

_____   _____

_____   _____

_____   _____

_____   _____

_____   _____

_____   _____

_____   _____

Open Communications

When Shirley's mother received the letter in China, Shirley felt frustrated because no one would tell her what was going on. In China, only the aged were considered wise, and children were not supposed to question or offer suggestions.

Have you ever felt the same way? Sometimes adults are afraid that children will not understand something, or that they are too young to handle responsibilities. Is there something you can do when you feel left out or unneeded? What do you think about the following ideas? Comment on each one.

1. Yell and scream to get their attention. _____

    _____

2. Ignore everyone back. _____

    _____

3. Tell them in a calm way how you feel. _____

    _____

4. Do something you know they would not approve of. _____

    _____

5. Ask other family members. _____

    _____

6. Cry and pout. _____

    _____

7. Seek the help of another adult such as a teacher. _____

    _____

8. Write them a letter. _____

    _____

Quiz Time!

1. If Shirley had calculated her age the way it is done in the United States, what age would she have been in February, 1947 in the U.S.? In China?

   _____

2. What does Mother mean when she tells Shirley that she is China's little ambassador?

   _____

3. What are two misunderstandings Shirley has on her first day of school?

   _____

4. Why do you think that as the weeks go by, Shirley finds herself more and more lonely?

   _____

5. What does "Shirley stood by like a hungry ghost" mean?

   _____

6. Why does Mother arrange for Shirley to take piano lessons?

   _____

7. Who is Toscanini and what is his job?

   _____

8. Why do you think Mabel changes her attitude towards Shirley?

   _____

9. Why do the children call Shirley "Jackie Robinson"?

   _____

10. What was Grandfather's lesson in telling the story of Wispy Whiskers?

    _____

What's Cooking?

Poor Shirley was really worried about eating when she learned that her mother would be responsible for cooking the meals. If each person in your class could have made her a menu for one day's meals, Shirley could have been set for a whole month!

If you were in charge of meals for a day, what would you make? Write out your menu here:

Breakfast

_____

_____

_____

Lunch

_____

_____

_____

Snacks

_____

_____

Dinner

_____

_____

_____

Choose one of your favorite dishes and write out the recipe for it. Draw a picture of what the dish should look like. You may want to demonstrate how to make your dish for the class, and then allow everyone a little taste. Make a class book of all the recipes and display it in the class for everyone to look at and copy down something they might want to try at home.

_____
            Name of Recipe

Ingredients:

Procedure:

Misunderstandings

Being unfamiliar with the language and customs of America, Shirley made some mistakes that were sometimes humorous, sometimes embarrassing, and sometimes painful. For example, Shirley thought that the long pole in the room was meant for punishing children, and she was certain that Mrs. Rappaport was going to use it on her. Instead, the pole was for opening the windows that were too high to reach. Another time when Shirley memorized her poem from a record, she found out it was actually the voices of some Disney characters. When Shirley tried to play stoop ball, not knowing enough numbers caused her to be left out of the game.

Certainly, misunderstandings happen to all of us, young and old, even when we are natives of a country. It is a part of the learning process. Sharing those experiences helps us to see that we are not alone. We can get to know one another better and give each other support.

Work with a partner for this activity. Tell your partner about something that happened to you as a result of a misunderstanding. It could be funny, embarrassing, or painful. After each partner has shared, then ask your partner if you may share the story with the rest of the class. Tell the rest of the class about your partner's experience.

Humorous

Embarrassing

Painful

Expressions

As Shirley learned English, she encountered some expressions that would cause anyone trouble unless they were explained. For example, she heard the others say "teacher's pet" and "apple shiner." Of course, in her mind she envisioned a dog belonging to the teacher or a person shining apples which have nothing to do with what they really mean. In English we have many such expressions and slang words or phrases that cannot be taken literally. Choose phrases from the following list. Write the phrases in the first column. Next to each phrase draw a picture of the literal translation. In the last column write the actual meaning.

run home (baseball)   In a pickle   on a roll
catch a fly (baseball)   music to my ears   beating around the bush
steal a base (baseball)   raining cats and dogs   In a jam
chip off the old block   climbing the walls   break the ice
sight for sore eyes   pay through the nose   on the fence

Phrase	Illustration	Actual Meaning

Being Accepted

Shirley found that establishing friendships was pretty difficult in her new home in Brooklyn. What were the reasons for the difficulty?

_____

_____

She understood that this was something she needed to work out by herself, and in time things did change. Mabel turned things around for her by becoming her supporter and teaching her how to play their games. Think about your own experiences with other children in school and/or your neighborhood. Do you identify more with Shirley's character or with Mabel's? Tell about yourself and an experience you have had that relates to one of the two characters.

In the Year of the Boar and Jackie Robinson

Quiz Time!

1. Why do you think Shirley says such strange words when the class says the Pledge of Allegiance?

   _____

2. What is Shirley referring to when she thinks that the other students call her "teacher's dog"?

   _____

3. How does Mrs. Rappaport compare the game of baseball to living in the United States?

   _____

   _____

4. What is "Dodger fever"?

   _____

5. Why do you think that Shirley has not written to Fourth Cousin in China in such a long time?

   _____

   _____

6. Why does Shirley feel it is important for Señora Rodriguez to go visit Nonnie?

   _____

   _____

7. What is the wonderful gift that Father bought Shirley?

   _____

   _____

8. What two things resulted from cleaning out the basement?

   _____

   _____

9. What is the one thing Father does not allow Shirley to do?

   _____

10. What happens when Shirley goes down to change the fuses?

   _____

   _____

Inventions

When Father took Shirley to the basement to clean things out, all she saw was a lot of junk. Father, on the other hand, saw a storehouse of treasure. Out of all the junk, Father was able to make something useful for each tenant in the building. He was using his inventive mind.

Be an inventor yourself. Do some brainstorming and make some inventions by thinking up new uses for old things. Here is a list of objects to start with. You can add to the list as you think of them.

paper clip	**toothbrush**	**sock**
straw	**chopsticks**	**plastic bag**
marbles	**balloon**	**fork**

There are different kinds of inventions. Usually, an invention is created to solve a problem. Sometimes an invention is simply an improvement on an existing device. However, an invention could also just be something unusual or fun, and not have any practical purpose at all.

Here are a few possible items that someone may have a need for:

* A page turner for musicians in an orchestra
* A tool for removing gum from the bottom of shoes
* Something to pick clothes up off the floor
* A bed maker

Add to this list with your own ideas. Then write down possible solutions, both practical and impractical. Choose one of the ideas to develop into a new invention. Describe the materials needed to build it, illustrate how it will look, and explain what it will do. Give your invention a name. Finally, build a model of your invention and have your own Invention Show to exhibit all your great ideas.

Invention: Illustration:

Materials:

Description:

24

The Brooklyn Dodgers

Here are some facts about the Brooklyn Dodgers. In small groups create as many questions as you can based on this information and use them to play a Brooklyn Dodger baseball game. Since winning the game depends on answering your questions, it will be to your advantage to think of questions that might stump your opponent. Write your questions on index cards. This page can serve as an answer key. Make a gameboard by drawing a baseball diamond with the bases and home plate marked. Pair groups up to be opposing teams. Each team has a chance to be "up" and must answer questions posed by the other team. When a person answers correctly, a marker is placed on first base. When the next person answers, the markers advance one base with a point being scored each time a marker reaches "home." An incorrect response is an "out" and three outs means the other team gets to be up. You may need to modify the rules to fit your own circumstances.

 The Dodgers first started playing in Brooklyn in 1884.

 The baseball team was named the Dodgers because the people of Brooklyn were always having to dodge trolley cars in the streets filled with tracks, especially to get to the game.

 In the early 1900's Charley Ebbets found a way to become the owner of the Dodgers in order to keep them in Brooklyn.

 In 1913 Ebbets Field, the brand new ballpark built by Ebbets, opened.

 The Dodgers won the pennant in 1916 and 1920, but not again until 1941.

 The Dodgers' first World Series was played against the Boston Red Sox in 1916.

 During the 1920's, the Dodgers' image fell and they were known as the "Daffiness Boys."

 In 1945 Branch Rickey, who was the general manager and part owner of the Dodgers at that time, signed Jackie Robinson to their Montreal farm team — the first step toward joining the Brooklyn Dodgers.

 In 1947 Jackie Robinson was promoted to the Brooklyn Dodgers. He was the first black American to play on a major league baseball team.

 Jackie Robinson was named Rookie of the Year in 1947 and was voted the league's Most Valuable Player in 1949.

 The Dodgers won the pennant in '41, '47, '49, '52, '53, '55, and '56 and played the New York Yankees in each of those seven World Series games.

 They won the World Series only once in 1955.

 Throughout all the years, the Dodgers were known affectionately as "de Bums" by loyal Brooklyn fans.

 In 1950 Walter O'Malley became owner and president of the Brooklyn Dodgers.

 Jackie Robinson retired from baseball in 1956.

 In 1957 the Brooklyn Dodgers moved to Los Angeles.

Understanding the Pledge

I pledge a lesson to the frog of the United States of America, and to the wee puppet for witches' hands. One Asian, in the vestibule, with little tea and just rice for all.

Each morning as the school day started, Shirley recited the Pledge of Allegiance with her class. Not knowing much English, Shirley said words she knew that sounded like what the rest of the class was saying. Perhaps if someone had explained the words to her, she would have realized how humorous her own words were.

The Pledge of Allegiance was written in 1892 by Francis Bellamy, who wrote it for children across the United States to recite in honor of the flag at the 400th anniversary celebration of Christopher Columbus's arrival. His salute was simple and only one sentence long:

I pledge allegiance to my flag and to the republic for which it stands —one Nation indivisible— with liberty and justice for all.

It was well-liked and soon children were saying it every morning to begin the school day. Since those first days, there have been two changes made to his pledge. First, in 1923 the words "my flag" were changed to "the flag of the United States of America" so that there would be no question about which flag. Then in 1954 Congress decided to add the words "under God" because Abraham Lincoln had used the phrase "this nation, under God" in his Gettysburg Address. (Do you see why Shirley's words do not include "under God"?)

Now the Pledge of Allegiance is 100 years old and it is still being used by everyone to show their support and love of their country.

Match Shirley's words with the real words and their meanings. Then rewrite the Pledge of Allegiance using the correct words on the back of this page.

a lesson = _____ means _____

frog = _____ means _____

wee puppet = _____ means _____

witches' hands = _____ means _____

One Asian = _____ means _____

in the vestibule = _____ means _____

little tea = _____ means _____

just rice = _____ means _____

republic	liberty	one nation	flag
allegiance	justice	indivisible	for which it stands

cannot be divided	one country	a symbol for	our red, white and blue
fairness	to be loyal	freedom	the kind of government we have

Doing Things for Others

Shirley's father thoughtfully made something for each tenant in the apartment building out of the things he cleaned out of the basement. As much as we intend to do something nice for someone else just as he did, we often become so involved in our own activities that we forget to take time for others.

Take time now to make some coupons to give to some of your favorite people. The coupons should show that you promise to do something for them at any time they wish to use their coupons. Carefully choose something you can do for them that they will truly appreciate. As you begin doing more and more for others, you will find that it becomes second nature, and making others feel good because of your good deed will make you feel good, too!

Quiz Time!

1. What is meant by "the dog days of August"?

   _____

2. Why does Shirley secretly throw out the herbal brew meant for Toscanini?

   _____

3. What fears cause Shirley to have the dream she has the night before school starts in September?

   _____

   _____

4. What characteristic draws Emily and Shirley together?

   _____

5. What is the great secret that Emily shares with Shirley?

   _____

6. What is Shirley's new job?

   _____

7. What do you think about Shirley's pay for one evening's work?

   _____

   _____

8. In what two ways does Shirley's plan to use the piggy bank money for bribery candy backfire?

   _____

   _____

9. What honor was given to Jackie Robinson?

   _____

10. Who wins the World Series that year?

   _____

Fun with Chinese Horoscopes

At the beginning of the book, the author says it is the Year of the Dog, 4645. The year 4645 is based on the Chinese lunar calendar which actually began in 2637 B.C. At that time, Emperor Huang Ti, who had reigned for 61 years, introduced a 60 year cycle that is made up of five 12-year cycles. Those five cycles correspond to the five elements: wood, fire, earth, metal, and water. Legend says that Lord Buddha called all the animals to him before he left the earth, but only 12 came to say good-bye. As a reward for coming, Buddha named a year after each animal in the order that it arrived. They were: (1) Rat, (2) Ox, (3) Tiger, (4) Rabbit, (5) Dragon, (6) Snake, (7) Horse, (8) Sheep, (9) Monkey, (10) Rooster, (11) Dog, and (12) Boar. The animals are said to influence the year's events as well as the personalities of those born in that year. The year of the Boar is said to be one of goodwill for everyone. It is a year filled with a feeling of abundance and much happiness. Does this match Shirley's year?

In the Chinese Lunar Calendar below, draw the animal for each year (it reads counterclockwise.) You will find the characteristics associated with each animal listed in the center. Does it seem to fit you?

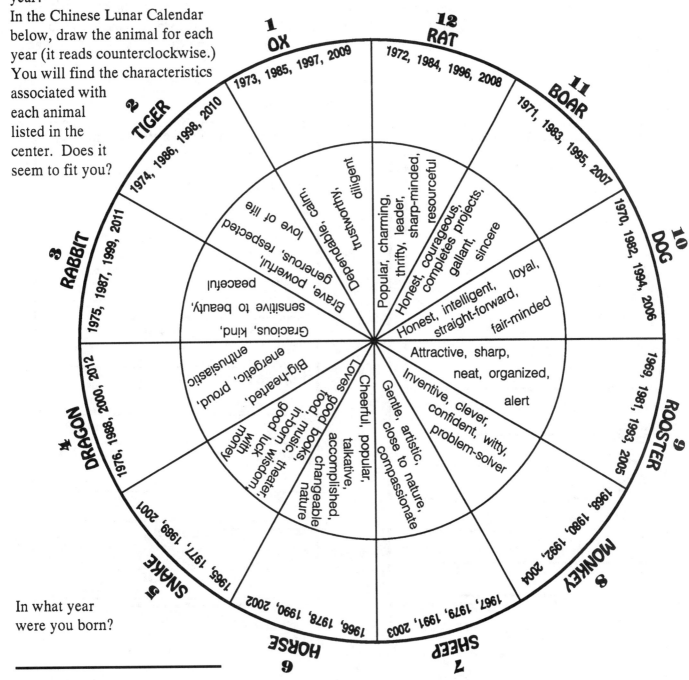

In what year were you born?

Hobbies and Interests

Shirley became a great fan of baseball and Jackie Robinson. In fact, all of America developed such an interest in baseball that baseball cards highlighting individual players became very popular in the 1950's. These cards came with bubble gum in each package, and kids collected and traded them, comparing sets to determine who had the biggest and best collection. Baseball cards have made a comeback in recent years, and the enthusiasm of the collectors may be just as great, if not greater, as the popularity they enjoyed in those early years.

Make a class set of student cards similar to those baseball cards, highlighting personal statistics and information about the hobbies and interests of each student. Working with a partner, collect information about the other person to create the card. Include a photo, either one provided by the student or use a polaroid camera and take one on the spot. Fill in the information, cut out the rectangles and glue them onto the front and back of a 3" x 5" (8 cm x 13 cm) index card. Make a display of the class Hall of Famers by hanging each card on a pin so that the cards can be easily removed to be read by everyone.

Photo

Name _____

Birthdate _____

Height _____

Family Members _____

_____

_____

Special hobby or favorite activity:

_____

Favorite sport to watch:

_____

Favorite subject:

_____

Favorite food:

_____

Greatest achievement:

_____

Funniest memory:

_____

_____

Happiest memory:

_____

_____

Most admired person:

_____

_____

Math—Finances

1. In Shirley's day, babysitting the triplets for a couple of hours earned her 3 dimes. Assuming this was two hours, how much was that per hour per child?_____

2. If you babysat the triplets today at $2.00 an hour per child, how much would you have earned for 2 hours of work? _____

3. How many times more money would you receive than Shirley did? _____

4. Shirley's father started a savings account for her with $5.00. If she earned 2% interest annually on that money, how much would she have gained after 1 year? (Remember that 2% is the same as .02 or $^2/_{100}$.) _____

5. How many times would Shirley have to babysit at 30¢ per job to earn another $5.00 to add to her account? _____

6. If Shirley received 10¢ each day for her lunch, how long would it have taken for her to replace the 30¢ she spent on candy for the triplets?_____

7. If Shirley wanted to buy a ticket to one of the Dodger games and it costs 55¢, how many hours must she babysit the triplets to earn enough money? _____

8. After one month of work, Shirley has saved up $1.20. She wants to treat herself and Emily at the candy store. What could she buy? Make 3 different combinations.

A. _____

B. _____

C. _____

Loyalty

Shirley and Emily became best friends. They did things together and shared everything. They even swore their loyalty to each other by swearing in blood. Being a real friend means a lot of different things, but above all, a true friendship is forever. Listen to the song, "That's What Friends Are For" recorded by Dionne Warwick by Arista Records.   Do you agree with the lyrics?

Think of some words and phrases that describe the essence of loyalty and friendship and fill in the acrostics.

L _____   **F** _____

O _____   **R** _____

Y _____   **I** _____

A _____   **E** _____

L _____   **N** _____

T _____   **D** _____

Y _____   **S** _____

                                     H _____

                                     I _____

                                     P _____

Quiz Time!

1. What is the Mid-Autumn Festival in China all about?

   _____

2. Why do you think the Wongs have forgotten the Mid-Autumn Festival?

   _____

3. What helps the Wongs to remember the festival?

   _____

4. Why do you think Shirley wishes to be the girl in Grandfather's story about the filial daughter and loving bride?

   _____

5. Why does Shirley hide her face in her hands when Emily asked that Shirley take her place in presenting the key to Jackie Robinson?

   _____

6. What is Mother's Christmas surprise?

   _____

7. What gifts does Shirley plan to give her new brother or sister?

   _____

8. What change did Jackie Robinson make in America?

   _____

9. Why does Shirley say that she could never be President of the United States?

   _____

10. Why is 1947 the year of "double happiness" for Shirley?

   _____

   _____

Mobiles

Throughout the year, Shirley has many different experiences. Each one could be brought to mind by naming an item related to it. For example, learning about going to America could be represented by a letter, and her love of baseball could be represented by a bat or ball. Use the pictures below or think of at least six other items associated with Shirley's experiences during that first year in Brooklyn. Draw, color, and cut out your items, making sure they will be large enough to hang on a mobile. Arrange them to make an attractive mobile display, using a hanger. Hang them from the ceiling to decorate the room.

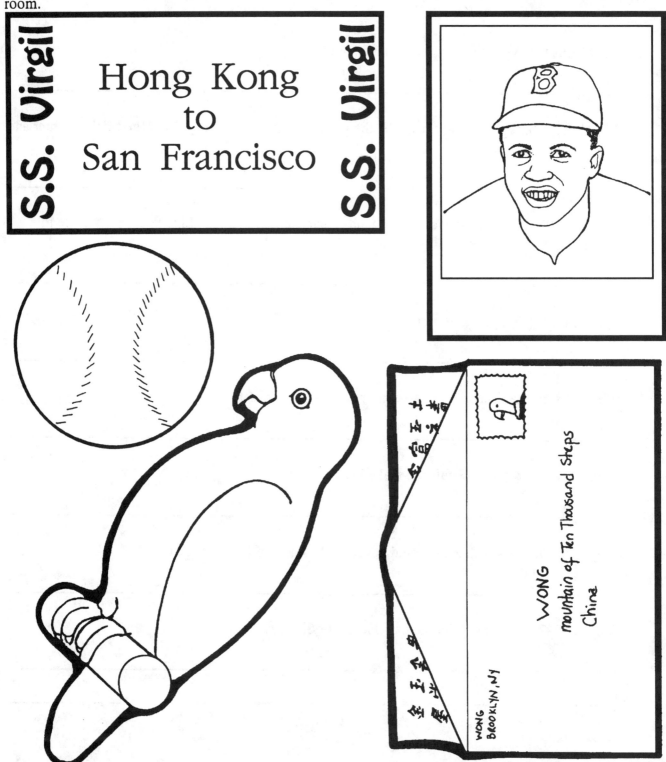

Fables

Grandfather had told Shirley the story about the farmer and his misfortunes which turned out to really be fortunes for him. Grandfather was trying to teach Shirley that things are not always what they seem. His story might be called a fable because it is a short fictitious narrative that has a moral or lesson. Usually fables have animals as characters, as in the well-known fables of Aesop. *A Chinese Zoo* by Demi is a collection of some Chinese fables that may be of interest to read as other examples.

From her experiences during her first year in Brooklyn, Shirley would probably have many lessons to teach that could be told in fable form. For example:

  * Strength is not always measured by muscle power.

  * Things are not always what they seem.

  * Some things take time.

  * Take time to teach others something new.

  * True friends are forever.

  * Beware of a jealous heart.

  * Stand up for what you believe.

  * It's OK to ask for help.

Working in small groups of three or four, think of your own moral or choose one of the above to create a fable for Shirley. Use animals as characters and draw an illustration to go with your story. Then act out your fable for the class.

So the bird asked the horse again.

"No I won't!" said the horse. "I don't want to."

American Contributors

Here are some facts about Jackie Robinson. Do you see any similarities between him and Shirley? In what ways are their experiences and personalities alike? Write something about Shirley to go with each of the facts about Jackie Robinson.

Jackie Robinson	**Shirley Temple Wong**

1. 1947 was his first year on a major league baseball team. _____

2. He was the first black person to play on a major league team. _____

3. People were prejudiced against him because he looked different. _____

4. He often felt very lonely on the team that first year. _____

5. He had to endure the hateful comments of white people. _____

6. His teammates and baseball fans changed their minds about him when he showed his skills and great courage. _____

7. He had one good friend on the team, Pee Wee Reese, who supported him. _____

8. He had much pride and desire to win. _____

9. He was honored as the Rookie of the Year. _____

10. He led the way for change in people's attitudes towards black Americans. _____

Jackie Robinson made significant contributions to society, not only as the first black player in major league baseball, but also as an advocate of civil rights and supporter of all minority groups. Among his many activities, he helped youngsters growing up in Harlem by teaching them about self-respect, ambition, and hope for the future. He also marched at the side of Martin Luther King, Jr. and was active politically.

There are many people who have made contributions to society in our country. Some are famous and some are not as well-known but just as important. Think of someone you believe is a positive influence in America today. It can be someone well-known throughout the country, someone known in your community, or someone known only to you.

Write a letter to that person inviting him/her to speak to your class. Explain why you admire him/her and how you and your class would benefit from the visit. Do a little research to find out the person's mailing address, then send your letter. Be sure to sign your full name and include your return address.

Heritage

Although Shirley understood the significance of being an American, a citizen of the United States, she also realized the importance of keeping her heritage, to know where she came from. Knowledge of our family history helps us understand ourselves better — why we look the way we do, and in part, why we think and act the way we do.

Do some family investigation and learn about the people in your past. Create a family booklet by filling in a page for each member. Fill in as much information as possible by talking to family members and/or looking up family records. Make a cover with your family name or something important to you on it. After you have finished, see if you can discover some of each of them in you, both inherited and learned.

Include information about your maternal great-grandparents, grandparents and mother, your paternal great-grandparents, grandparents, father, and of course, a page about you.

My Family

Name: _____

Relationship: _____

Birthplace: _____

Grew up in: _____

Hair color: _____

Eye color: _____

Distinctive physical trait: _____

_____

Distinctive personality trait: _____

_____

Special skills and/or interests: _____

_____

_____

_____

Book Report Ideas

There are numerous ways to do a book report. After you have finished reading *In the Year of the Boar and Jackie Robinson*, choose one method of reporting that interests you. It may be a way that your teacher suggests, an idea of your own, or one of the ways below.

- **Board Game**

  Make a board game based on the events of *In the Year of the Boar and Jackie Robinson*. Lay out the spaces on a piece of construction paper or tag board. You might want to add comments here and there on the spaces for interest, such as Lose one turn, Go back 3 spaces, or Move forward 1 space. Then decorate around the spaces with scenes from the book. Make a set of at least 25 game cards, each with a question about the story. Make an answer key on a separate sheet of paper in order to check responses during the game. You will need a die and colored markers for each player. To play, the players must answer a question correctly in order to roll the die and move. The first person to reach the Finish is the winner!

- **Filmstrip**

  Make a filmstrip or "roller movie" of the story of *In the Year of the Boar and Jackie Robinson*. Draw pictures of all the significant events of the story and "roll it" as you narrate. If blank filmstrips are available, use colored markers for drawing and present your work on the screen. If not, use a roll of paper such as computer paper rolled onto a dowel on each end. Cut a "screen" into an appropriate size box. Insert the dowels on the top and bottom from the back so that they can be turned to create a "roller movie" which can be narrated.

- **Literary Critic**

  Be a literary critic and write a book review of *In the Year of the Boar and Jackie Robinson*. Include a brief summary of the story and your opinion on the strengths and weaknesses of the plot, characters, and writing style. Tell whether or not you recommend this book to other readers.

- **Book Jacket**

  You are the publisher of the book *In the Year of the Boar and Jackie Robinson*. Design a book jacket that will attract attention and encourage people to pick up the book and want to read it.

- **TV Commercial**

  With other students, as many as necessary, create and perform a TV commercial to sell the book. Make your commercial entertaining and to the point.

- **Letter to the Author**

  Write a letter to Bette Bao Lord and tell her what you thought about *In the Year of the Boar and Jackie Robinson*. Include specific points about what you liked most or least. Ask any questions that came to mind as you read the book. You may want to ask questions about being a writer and how she got the idea for this story. After your teacher has read it, and you have made your writing the best it can be, send it to her in care of the publishing company.

- **Performing**

  Act out a scene from *In the Year of the Boar and Jackie Robinson*. You may need to ask some fellow students to help you out by being other characters. Explain why you chose the scene and why it is important to the story.

- **Model**

  Construct a 3-dimensional model of your favorite scene from *In the Year of the Boar and Jackie Robinson*. Give an oral explanation of the scene and why you chose it.

Research Ideas

Describe three things you read about in *In the Year of the Boar and Jackie Robinson* that you would like to learn more about.

1. _____

2. _____

3. _____

Although *In the Year of the Boar and Jackie Robinson* is a fictional story, there are many ideas and facts that bring up questions and suggest topics for further study. Researching and developing a better understanding of such topics enhance one's appreciation for the book and its author.

Work in groups to research one or more of the areas you named above, or the areas that are mentioned below. Share your findings with the rest of the class in any appropriate form of oral presentation.

- Chinese festivals and celebrations
- Chinese lunar calendar
- Chinese customs and traditions
- Changes in China in the past 50 years
- History of the Pledge of Allegiance
- Naturalization process
- History of baseball
- Famous baseball players
- Civil Rights Movement
- Music
  - Instruments
  - Orchestras
  - Chamber music
  - Reading music
- Inventors and their inventions
- American heroes
- Duties of an ambassador
- Opportunities in America
- Changes in the value of the dollar
- Map making
- Hobbies

Changes

As we follow Shirley Temple Wong through her first year in America, she goes through many changes as a result of the events and experiences she encounters. For each month of the year describe one event that occurs and explain how it affects Shirley.

January

Event: _____

Effect: _____

February

Event: _____

Effect: _____

March

Event: _____

Effect: _____

April

Event: _____

Effect: _____

May

Event: _____

Effect: _____

June

Event: _____

Effect: _____

July

Event: _____

Effect: _____

August

Event: _____

Effect: _____

September

Event: _____

Effect: _____

October

Event: _____

Effect: _____

November

Event: _____

Effect: _____

December

Event: _____

Effect: _____

Changes *(cont.)*

What do you think happened to Shirley Temple Wong in the years that followed? Use your imagination and what you know of her personality to describe what might have become of her in the 30 years following 1947. What happened to her? What things did she do? Was she happy? Write your story using the cover below or design one of your own.

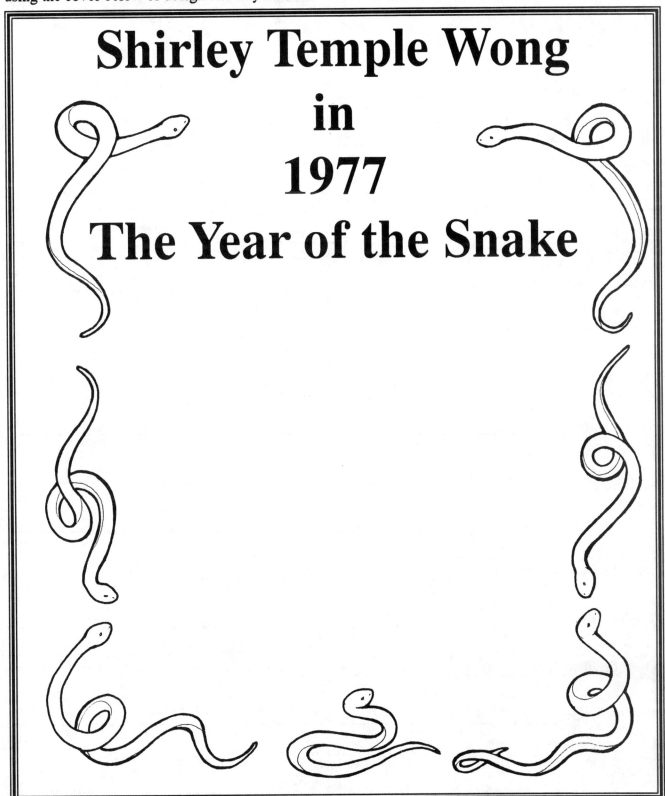

Shirley Temple Wong
in
1977
The Year of the Snake

In the Year of the Boar and Jackie Robinson

Changes *(cont.)*

If this same story were set in the present year, what details would need to be changed to make it realistic and consistent with the times? Write your ideas on the lines following each detail.

Bandit's new American name: _____

Mode of travel from China to the U.S.: _____

City Shirley moves to: _____

Modern appliances: _____

Who would cook: _____

What would Shirley go to buy for her father: _____

Games and activities of the children: _____

Candies found in the store: _____

Major sport: _____

Sport's hero: _____

Way to follow the sport games: _____

Pay for babysitting: _____

Cost of a week's groceries: _____

The Year of the: _____

Other details: _____

New book title: _____

42

Unit Test

Matching: Match the quotes with the characters who said them.

Emily	Jackie Robinson	Grandfather	Mrs. Rappaport	Father

1. _____ ". . . Remember always the tale of Wispy Whiskers, who did not cry when his beautiful stallion ran away. All his neighbors, though, were certain that it was a sign from heaven of his ill fortune. . . ."

2. _____ "Yes. It is not too early to plan. College is expensive, but it is the most valuable treasure a person can have. With a proper education, you can aspire to do anything you desire in America. Be a doctor or a teacher or . . ."

3. _____ "Hooray for the sister of our future President, Shirley Temple Wong, the American!"

4. _____ "In our national pastime, each player is a member of a team, but when he comes to bat, he stands alone. One man. Many opportunities. For no matter how far behind, how late in the game, he, by himself, can make a difference. He can change what has been. He can make it a new ball game. . . ."

5. _____ "That's what friends are for."

True or False: Write true or false next to each statement below.

1. _____ Shirley had a hard time at school on her first day because something was wrong with her eyes.

2. _____ The girl who gave Shirley two black eyes became one of her best friends.

3. _____ Sean, Seamus, and Stephen were three of the boys in Shirley's class.

4. _____ The Wongs took care of the apartment house for free while Señora Rodriguez went to visit her daughter.

5. _____ *In the Year of the Boar and Jackie Robinson* contains some historical facts.

Short Answer: Provide a short answer for each of these questions.

1. Why did Bandit take Precious Coins with her to see Grandmother? _____

_____

2. What do you think about the way Shirley handled her confrontation with Mabel? _____

_____

3. Why had Father screamed the night the lights went out? _____

_____

4. Who won the World Series in 1947? _____

_____

5. Why is this book called *In the Year of the Boar and Jackie Robinson*? _____

_____

Essay: Answer these essay questions on the back of this paper.

1. Is the story of Shirley Temple Wong believable? Give at least three examples from the book to support your position.

2. Compare and contrast Shirley's experiences in the first half of the year to the second half of the year. Use specific examples.

Response

Explain the meaning of the following quotations from *In the Year of the Boar and Jackie Robinson*.

January: *"Bandit felt as if she had sprouted a second head, and they were all determined to ignore politely the unsightly growth."*

February: *"Must we eat out for every meal? Shirley wondered."*

March: *"Shirley flinched when the teacher went straight to the long mean pole."*

April: *"Day by day, week by week, little by little Shirley shrank until she was no more."*

April: *"When the lunch bell sounded, Shirley raced to be the first in line and waited impatiently for the new girl."*

May: *"Oh no! She had done the wrong thing. Now even her new friend was angry. 'Go home,' her teammates shouted. 'Go home.' "*

May: *"Until that day, Shirley had never really understood something Grandfather had told her many times. 'Things are not what they seem,' he had said. 'Good can be bad. Bad can be good. Sadness can be happiness. Joy, sorrow.' "*

June: *"She felt as if she had the power of ten tigers, as if she had grown as tall as the Statue of Liberty."*

July: *"In fact, they welcomed the mayhem that emanated from the talking box as if it were a plague of locusts at harvest time."*

August: *". . . It's just another wonderful engine made in America."*

August: *"Pocketing the keys, she felt her way along the walls. Was it her imagination, or did they feel wet and sticky, like blood?"*

September: *"She came to a fork in the road, one she remembered well, but now she could not tell which path was the way home. She looked to the east and thought she heard her mother call, 'This way. This way.' She looked to the west and thought she heard her father call, 'This way. This way.' Confused, she did not know how to choose."*

September: *"A secret, like a chore, always seems to lead to another, one even more troublesome than the first."*

October: *"Wait until next year, everyone said. Only next year seemed as far away as a balloon lost in summer skies."*

November: *" 'I wish I were the girl in Grandfather's story.' "*

December: *"What a star-spangled Christmas this is! she thought."*

Conversations

Work in size-appropriate groups to write and perform the conversations that might have occurred in each of the following situations.

* Grandfather, Grandmother, and Mother have a discussion about the letter from Father. (3 people)

* Mr. Tan and Mr. Hu tell Mr. Lin and Mr. Koo what happened to Shirley when she left to buy cigarettes for her father. (4 people)

* The students in Mrs. Rappaport's class talk among themselves about the new girl, Shirley, on her first day at school. (2 or more people)

* Shirley tells her mother and father about her first piano lesson with Señora Rodriguez. (3 people)

* Members of the clan in China discuss how their family in America might be doing. (2 or more people)

* Father talks to Mother and Shirley about why he decided to live in America. (3 people)

* Shirley explains to Señora Rodriguez why she loves baseball so much. (2 people)

* The tenants of the apartment house talk about what they think of the their new temporary landlord, Mr. Wong. (5 people)

* Mrs. Reilly tells some of the other members of her church about her new babysitter, Shirley. (2 or more people)

* Shirley talks to Mother about her new best friend, Emily. (2 people)

* Mr. P. tells his wife about how much Shirley has changed since she first came to his store on her first day of school. (2 people)

* Getting the moon cakes ready to send to America, Grandfather and Grandmother talk about the Moon Festival and about their children. (2 people)

* After the Assembly, Mabel, Emily, and Shirley talk about the past year, how they met and their first impressions. (3 people)

* Shirley sees her Grandfather in a dream and talks to him about her new life. (2 people)

* Create your own conversation idea for the characters of *In the Year of the Boar and Jackie Robinson.*

Bibliography

Commire, Anne, Editor. *Something About the Author, Vol. 58.* (Gale Research, Inc., 1990)

Demi. *A Chinese Zoo: Fables and Proverbs.* (Harcourt Brace Jovanovich, 1987)

Davidson, Margaret. *The Story of Jackie Robinson, Bravest Man in Baseball.* (Dell Publishing, 1988)

Gardner, Robert. *Experimenting with Inventions.* (Franklin Watts, 1990)

Golenbock, Peter. *Bums: An Oral History of the Brooklyn Dodgers.* (G. P. Putnam's Sons, 1984)

Honig, Donald. *The Brooklyn Dodgers: An Illustrated Tribute.* (St. Martin's Press, 1981)

Lau, Theodora. *The Handbook of Chinese Horoscopes.* (Harper Colophon Books, 1979)

Marsh, Susan. *All About Maps and Mapmaking.* (Random House, 1963)

May, Hal, Editor. *Contemporary Authors, Vol. 107.* (Gale Research Company, 1983)

Mims, Forrest M., III. *Number Machines.* (David McKay Company, Inc., 1977)

Swanson, June. *I Pledge Allegiance.* (Carolrhoda Books, 1990)

Weiss, Harvey. *How to Be an Inventor.* (Thomas Y. Crowell, 1980)

Other Books About the Chinese Culture

Mahy, Margaret. *The Seven Chinese Brothers.* (Scholastic, 1990)

Say, Allen. *El Chino.* (Houghton, 1990)

Wang, Rosalind. *The Fourth Question: A Chinese Tale.* (Holiday House, 1991)

Yee, Paul. *Tales from Gold Mountain: Stories of the Chinese in the New World.* (Macmillan, 1990)

Yen, Clara. *Why Rat Comes First.* (Children's Book Press, 1991)

Yep, Lawrence. *The Lost Garden.* (Julian Messner, 1991)

Answer Key

Page 12

1. U.S. bald eagle.
2. Mother smiled, Grandmother cried, and Grandfather became angry.
3. Only aged were considered wise.
4. Grandmother had always said that breaking something during the holidays would bring bad luck for the rest of the year.
5. Cowboys and Indians everywhere, warm puppies (hot dogs) and raw meat (hamburgers) for food, uncivilized people.
6. See Chapter 1.
7. It was the only name she knew besides Uncle Sam.
8. Brooklyn, New York; by boat and train.
9. See Chapter 2.
10. She couldn't find her way home.

Page 18

1. 8 yrs.; 10 yrs.
2. Because Shirley might be the only Chinese some people would ever meet, they will form their opinion of all Chinese based on how she acted, so she must be the best model.
3. Winking; long pole.
4. Accept appropriate responses.
5. She wanted to be part of the group, but others did not seem to see her.
6. She wanted to cheer Shirley up by letting her do something that she, herself, had always wanted to do.
7. Señora Rodriguez's parrot who called for notes to be played on the piano.
8. Accept any reasonable response.
9. She made it across home plate.
10. Things are not always what they seem.

Page 23

1. Accept any appropriate response.
2. She was thinking of "teacher's pet."
3. See Chapter 6.
4. Being obsessed with Dodger baseball.
5. She was busy with her new life and found it harder to remember her Chinese.

6. Family is important.
7. Sofa-bed.
8. Everyone received a gift and Shirley learned how things work and how to fix them.
9. Paint the halls.
10. She unknowingly touched the wet paint and put hand prints over all the walls.

Page 26

a lesson = allegiance means to be loyal

frog = flag means our red, white and blue

wee puppet = republic means the kind of government we have

witches' hands = for which it stands means a symbol for

One Asian = one nation means one country

in the vestibule = indivisible means cannot be divided

little tea = liberty means freedom

just rice = justice means fairness

Page 28

1. The hottest days at the end of August.
2. She thought he might grow long, black Chinese hair.
3. She was changing and losing her Chinese heritage.
4. Their no-nonsense attitude, both new, both had braids.
5. They looked at *Gray's Anatomy*.
6. Babysitting Mrs. O'Reilly's triplets.
7. Accept any appropriate response.
8. She felt guilty for having deceived her parents, and the boys acted worse when there was no candy, causing her to miss the important pennant game.
9. Rookie of the Year.
10. New York Yankees.

Page 31

1. 5¢ 2. $12.00 3. 40 times 4. 10¢ 5. 17 times (16.67) 6. 3 days 7. 4 hours (3.67) 8. Accept appropriate combinations.

Answer Key *(cont.)*

Page 33

1. Commemoration of the fullest moon of the year and celebration of the family.
2. It is not celebrated in the United States and everyone was busy.
3. Grandfather sent traditional moon cakes.
4. She wanted to be two people at the same time — the daughter in America and the granddaughter in China.
5. She was ashamed for having felt jealous of Emily.
6. She was expecting a baby.
7. She would teach him Chinese and tell him about life in Chungking and especially about their family there.
8. He was the first black American to play major league baseball.
9. She was not born in the United States.
10. She became an American and she met Jackie Robinson.

Page 40

Although students may choose different events, here are some possible responses:

January: Letter arrives from Father; Excited about moving to America.

February: Gets lost in Brooklyn; It's OK to make mistakes — we learn and improve from them.

March: First day in school; Learning a new language and new customs is difficult.

April: No one to talk to and do things with; Having a friend would make all the difference.

May: Gets into a fight with Mabel; Things are not always what they seem.

June: Learns about Jackie Robinson; America is land of opportunity for everyone.

July: Señora Rodriguez wants to visit Nonnie; Family ties are important.

August: Cleaning out the basement; Imagination can make things out of what they are not.

September: Has a new job; A secret tends to grow.

October: Dodgers play in World Series; Sense of team spirit, loyal fan.

November: Grandfather sends moon cakes; Feels torn between two lives.

December: Meets Jackie Robinson; Pride in being an American.

Page 43

Matching:
1. Grandfather
2. Father
3. Jackie Robinson
4. Mrs. Rappaport
5. Emily

True/False:
1. False
2. True
3. False
4. False
5. True

Short Answer:
1. She thought Grandmother would not be as angry if Precious Coins were there to cry for her.
2. Accept any appropriate response.
3. He saw that Shirley had put handprints all over the walls.
4. The New York Yankees.
5. 1947 is called the Year of the Boar by the Chinese; it was Jackie Robinson's year; and both were important to Shirley.

Essays: Accept any well-supported answer.